Sales Forecasting

Monograph Series #10

Sales Forecasting

George C. Michael
Glenn Bozell & Jacobs, Inc.

AMERICAN
MARKETING
ASSOCIATION

222 South Riverside Plaza • Chicago, Illinois 60606 • (312) 648-0536

Cover Design by Mary Jo Krysinski

Library of Congress Cataloging in Publication Data

Michael, George C.
    Sales forecasting.

    (Monograph series - American Marketing Association ;
no. 10)
    Bibliography: p.
    1. Sales forecasting. I. Title. II. Series:
American Marketing Association. Monographs series - Amer-
ican Marketing Association ; 10.
HF5415.2.M44   658.8'18   79-9532
ISBN 0-87757-128-7

TABLE OF CONTENTS

Introduction iv

   I. Forecasting Problems 1

  II. Forecasting Decision-Making. 5

 III. The Basic Methods 7

 IV. Judgmental Techniques. 9

  V. Time Series Techniques. 17

 VI. Causal Techniques. 23

 VII. Comparison of Techniques 33

VIII. Forecasting Effectiveness 37

 IX. Summary. 39

INTRODUCTION

This monograph on forecasting is unique in several ways. First, its orientation is strictly that of business decision-makers who have need of forecasts, yet may be uncomfortable with forecasting as a process. Second, the problems that make decision-makers uncomfortable with forecasts are openly discussed, and advice is given to minimize these problems. Third, five forecasting questions are posed that will allow decision-makers to approach forecasting situations methodically. Finally, a handy Forecasting Decision Matrix (page 34) has been developed that allows decision-makers to compare at a glance the major forecasting techniques against the criteria posed by the five forecasting questions.

George C. Michael
June 1979

CHAPTER I

FORECASTING PROBLEMS

One of the most important activities in any business is sales forecasting. Yet, there is probably no other activity that is as shrouded in mystery and as misunderstood as forecasting. This situation does not need to be so. Given perspective and understanding, decision-makers can act thoughtfully and knowingly in choosing the most effective technique to develop sales forecasts.

Before specific techniques are discussed and compared, however, decision-makers should understand why they may currently feel uneasy about forecasting. The basic problems are listed as follows and then discussed in detail:

- Forecasting has a certain *mystique* to it that puts off typical decision-makers uninitiated in the various aspects of forecasting.

- Forecasts and forecasting people tend to promise—intentionally at times, but usually unintentionally—more *accuracy* than can be delivered.

- Forecasts are not always developed with *consistency* in mind; confusion can result.

- Forecasting is one of the few purely staff functions, yet it greatly impacts the line organization with little *accountability* to it.

- The *implementation* of forecasts is often in the form of sales achievement results, which may or may not reflect the true nature of forecasts as best estimates.

Problem: Forecasting Mystique

There is no question that forecasting has a mystique to it. This mystique comes from four primary sources:

1

- Forecasting now encompasses a myriad of techniques, ranging from very simple, traditional ones to very complex, sophisticated ones. Keeping current on all these techniques is no easy task.

- The forecasting experts are not very cummunicative. Too often the experts do not bother to explain why a particular technique is more appropriate than another. Also, the experts tend to speak in forecasting jargon, practically a foreign language to business people not accustomed to the jargon.

- Many forecast techniques have unusual names. These names aren't necessarily descriptive or helpful to the decision-maker. For example, some of the names decision-makers must cope with are as follows: Delphi, exponential smoothing, and Box-Jenkins. These names are formidable and hardly contribute to a feeling of comfort for decision-makers facing a forecasting situation.

- Perhaps the greatest villain for decision-makers is the computer. The more recently developed techniques require a computer. Decision-makers see little more than a print-out and a final forecast with no evidence, such as graphs, calculations, and formulas, showing how the input data were handled.

Problem: Forecasting Accuracy

Another area of uneasiness, and of a great deal of frustration, for decision-makers is the lack of accuracy of many forecasts—a lack of accuracy which comes in several forms.

Because forecasts are made under a set of assumptions, which may or may not be accurate, forecasts are notorious for failing to match actual results. These types of errors can be minimized but they will never be entirely avoided because working with the future will always involve uncertainty.

In another sense almost all forecasts are wrong. If sales of a certain product are predicted to be 62,000 units, and actual sales are 62,064, the forecast was wrong—not in a way meaningful to decision-making, perhaps, but nevertheless, "inaccurate." This type of inaccuracy comes from an *over-preciseness* that forecasters tend to promise. Forecasts are usually stated in very rigid forms. Some may be rounded to the nearest thousandth unit, but still an exact number is there. This preciseness may be easier to work with initially; later, however, it haunts both forecaster and forecast user.

Problem: Forecasting Consistency

A practice that frustrates those involved in forecasting is the continual subjective modifications made by both forecasters and decision-makers to forecast data and results. These modifications range from adjusting or throwing out data because of unusual variations to adjusting results because of a known bias by one of the participants in the forecasting process. While these modifications may make forecasts more accurate, the motive for these modifications is often difficult to understand and explain.

Problem: Forecasting Accountability

Another problem area is the indefinite organizational accountability associated with forecasting. Rare is the business that allows a decision maker to develop a forecast and then live with it. Many companies, in fact, distinctly separate forecasting responsibility from line responsibility. Forecasting and the line organization become two different functions—one area is responsible for *developing* the forecast and another area is responsible for *achieving* the forecast. Curiously, some forecasters and decision-makers find a benefit in this division of responsibility, as each can attempt to avoid possible blame when actual sales do not meet the level forecast by claiming "the forecast was too high" or "the sales people didn't do their job" as appropriate.

Problem: Forecasting Implementation

Related to forecasting accountability problems are problems with the implementation of forecasts as sales quotas, targets or goals. Forecasts are not the same as quotas, targets or goals. Forecasts are the best estimates of sales in a given period. There is nothing wrong with taking forecasts, adjusting them, if desirable, and using them as benchmarks to measure sales achievements. However, the distinction between forecasts and sales quotas, targets, and goals is rarely made and often leads to misunderstanding and consternation in both forecasters and sales managers.

CHAPTER II

FORECASTING DECISION-MAKING

Decision-makers can minimize most of the possible forecasting problems by knowledgeably choosing the right technique. Too often, the decision-maker does not have a choice in selecting a forecasting technique or does not have the knowledge to select the right one.

Choosing the Right Technique

Most of the time a company will either develop or buy a forecasting technique and then use it. For most of the forecasts needed by the company, this technique probably suffices. However, for some others the usual technique is probably not effective, being either too expensive or, more often, not yielding accurate enough results. Unfortunately, these exceptional situations in which the company's usual technique is not appropriate are the most important ones. Common examples where special forecasts and forecasting techniques are needed are cases involving introduction of a new product, long-term capital expenditures, and product phase-outs.

The Five Forecasting Questions

Instead of choosing a forecasting technique by using whatever may be available, decision-makers should ask questions to determine what is appropriate. For decision-makers to select the most appropriate forecasting technique, five questions need to be asked and answered:

Accuracy: Why Do You Need the Forecast? The answer to this question summarizes the background information needed to choose the most appropriate technique. Here, a decision is made as to *how accurate* the forecast needs to be. Certainly, the accuracy for a first-year new product sales forecast is much more critical than that for a one-week, reorder forecast of a single retail sales unit. Different techniques with different degrees of accuracy are appropriate under different conditions.

Cost: How Much Money is Involved? By knowing *how much money is involved* in the situation, the decision-maker knows *how much money it is appropriate to spend* to develop the forecast. Clearly, since forecasting techniques vary in cost from almost no cost to almost prohibitive in all but the most unusual situations, this question is very important.

Timing: When Will the Forecast be Used? Just as forecasting techniques vary in costs, they also vary in the length of time they remain useful. Decision-makers should notice that the question asks when the forecast will be *used*, not *desired*. If a forecast is developed early in the project and then not used until the end of the project, the forecast may have become outdated and inaccurate. Either an updated forecast is needed in such situations, or the forecast development should be delayed until the forecast is actually needed.

Form: Who Will Use the Forecast? Forecasts can be stated in many different forms. A forecast prepared for the sales force should be different in form than one prepared for the corporate economist. Unfortunately, issuing forecasts in a single form has been standard practice for forecasters. Since different techniques result in forecasts with different forms, the *communication issues for the end users* should be considered.

Data: How Much Are Available? Techniques vary in the amount of data they require. By accessing the *amount of relevant data already available*, decision-makers will be able to focus on the appropriate technique more easily.

CHAPTER III

THE BASIC METHODS

Having asked and answered the five forecasting questions of *accuracy, cost, timing, form,* and *data,* decision-makers should then be ready to choose the most appropriate forecasting techniques. Each major technique can be placed into one of three categories: judgmental, time series, or causal techniques. These three categories vary in the *type of data that is required*—qualitative as opposed to quantitative—and *how the data are used.*

Each of the three categories of forecasting techniques is discussed in detail in the following three sections. Within each category, each technique is described and then discussed with respect to the five forecasting questions of accuracy, cost, timeliness, form of output, and data required. Applications of use are then given for each technique.

CHAPTER IV

JUDGMENTAL TECHNIQUES

Judgmental techniques use qualitative data, relying primarily on the judgments of those participating in the forecasting process. Judgmental techniques are attempts to bring objectivity to non-structured situations and to treat relevant information in an orderly, systematic way. Information about the past may or may not be included, depending on the circumstances. As expected, judgmental techniques are subjective in nature and vary considerably from use to use.

The following judgmental techniques are discussed:

- Case History/Analogy

- Expert Opinion

- Delphi

- Consensus Opinion

- Survey of Users

- Heuristic Forecasting

Case History/Analogy

Description. One method often used to forecast the success of a new product and its consequent growth is to compare it with similar products already on the market. Research into successes and failures of established products can provide the forecaster with good estimates of demand. Case analogies are especially helpful when data are scarce—particularly when a product is first introduced in a market. They enable a marketer to turn human judgment into quantitative estimates.

Accuracy. Short term: The case history/analogy method usually is not effective in the very immediate short term (up

9

to three months), but it is reasonably effective after that point. Long term: The method is rated good to fair in the long run.

Cost. The cost of developing a case history is quite variable. With the use of a computer to do a search, the cost of case history forecasting can mount quickly. However, it is not necessary to use a computer—in which case the costs would center on the number of man-hours needed. Minimum costs usually exceed $1,000 in either case.

Timing. To develop an application of a case history and make an accurate forecast, at least one month is normally required. Data gathering is the most time-consuming phase of the process.

Form of Forecast. The information garnered from this approach is actually produced in rather sketchy form. It is somewhat vague in that so much is dependent on human judgment. The information is rated only fair in identifying marketing turning points.

Data Required. The data required include several years' history of one or more products similar to the one in question.

Applications. The case history/analogy method is best used for forecasts of long-range and new product sales and forecasts of profit margins. An example of when a sales history/analogy would be appropriate is in projecting the market for video home recording systems, based on the advance of color televisions over black-and-white televisions.

Expert Opinion

Description. Characterized by subjective estimates and imagination, this method uses personal insights, judgment, and facts about different scenarios for the future. A common justification for the use of this method is that a company finds it expedient to capitalize on the experience and knowledge of those individuals who are in good positions to judge the course of future product sales.

Judgmental forecasts such as this are sometimes used as checks on market predictions obtained in other ways. The expert opinion approach may be favored for many different reasons, such as low cost, a relatively stable sales volume and a low risk of serious error, or a scarcity of market data needed for other approaches.

Accuracy. Short term: Accuracy is considered fair with this approach; too much can go wrong with forecasts based on human judgment. Long term: also considered fair.

Cost. The added cost of forecasting with the use of a computer is minimal, and the experts are often on the corporation's payroll as executives or consultants.

Timing. Of all judgmental approaches, the expert opinion takes the least amount of time. A reasonable estimate of the time required to make a forecast using this method is one week or more.

Form of Forecast. As with the case history method, the output format of the expert opinion approach is rather vague. For application in the identification of market turning points, this method is considered poor.

Data Required. Several possible scenarios for the future prepared by different experts, based on past events, are all that is required.

Applications. Data obtained from the expert opinion approach are best applied to long-range and new product forecasts, as well as profit-margin forecasts. The data are best used in conjunction with other scientific methods, unless such data are not available. Often, they are used when the scarcity of data and time makes other methods unfeasible.

Delphi

Description. The Delphi technique is a group forecasting method adjusted to eliminate the bandwagon effect of majority opinion. The use of anonymous questionnaires reduces the effects of dominant individuals, whose presence usually leads to group pressure.

A panel of experts is questioned in stages. The results of each stage are fed back to each panelist so that he can revise his answers in light of what the entire group thought on that round. Any information available to some and not to others is thereby passed on so that all have access to the information needed for forecasting.

Rather than requiring the group to arrive at a consensus in the end, group opinion is taken to be a statistical average of the final opinions of the individual members. Obviously, the value of a Delphi exercise depends a great deal on how well the panelists are chosen.

Accuracy. Short term: Generally, this method is applied in medium- to long-term situations, although it can yield good results even in the short term. Long term: rated fair to very good.

11

Cost. The cost of the executives' time is the major expense. Who makes up the panel and how many rounds are built into the process determine exact costs.

Timing. Over two months is usually required to make an accurate forecast.

Form of Forecast. As in any judgmental forecast, there are pitfalls in relying solely on this form of prediction. Even though the Delphi method is highly disciplined, results are bound to be somewhat vague. Nevertheless, past users of Delphi studies have reported their relative satisfaction with the results obtained.

Data Required. A coordinator is needed to develop and issue the questionnaires in sequence, to edit them, and to consolidate the panelists' responses.

Applications. Although this method is applicable to long-range and new product sales, it has often been used to give clues to the general context and timing of future technological and other events that might affect an entire industry or market. It is also used for "trend impact analysis"—attempts to modify trend projections in light of other trends or events that could alter the course of the trend—and "cross impact analysis"—attempts to determine the likelihood of an event while considering the possible interactions with other events.

One major corporation used this method to develop a ten-year market forecast for certain new components it was planning to manufacture and got excellent results. The study took almost a year to complete and used a three-phase approach. The information was obtained from over 40 experts. The panelists were reported to be highly committed to the project. The corporation was impressed with the rationales that the panelists gave for their answers and with their ability to move toward a consensus.

Consensus Opinion

Description. Forecasts reached by combining the views of key people in a business can often provide a better forecast than might be made by a single predictor. Basically, two methods are used:

- *Panel*—Key executives are brought together in a panel situation to air forecasting differences and arrive at a consensus. Open communication is encouraged and

12

there is no secrecy. Possible problems with this method include the possibilities of giving too much weight to opinion, taking up too much executive time, and according equal weight to the estimates of all forecasters no matter how inaccurate their predictions have been in the past. Also, panels are subject to the "bandwagon effect," which means that a true consensus is not always reached.

- *Sales Force Estimation*—Many managements turn to members of the field sales force for help in forecasting because they are usually better positioned than anyone else in a company to judge the near-term outlook for sales in their areas. Often sales representatives are polled formally as to their area sales predictions, which may reflect in part the results of their quizzing customers and prospects regarding purchase plans. Estimates prepared by sales representatives are checked and revised at higher levels, so that the final forecast is the result of what has been called a "jury of sales executive opinion."

One possible problem with this method concerns the accuracy of a sales force estimate, taking into account that sales quotas are linked to sales forecasts and that compensation may be determined by sales performance with regard to these quotas. There is most likely a tendency for sales representatives to underestimate future sales.

Accuracy. Short term: With few exceptions, estimates of future sales based on consensus opinion are best used for very short-range planning. Long term: Forecasts for the long term are best obtained by other methods. Consensus opinion is considered poor for any time period beyond two years.

Cost. Executive and sales force time should be considered when using this method. Aside from the cost of management time, consensus opinion is a relatively inexpensive method.

Timing. A two-week period is usually required for a consensus of opinion estimate. This is one of the quickest of the qualitative forecasting techniques.

Form of Forecast. Because a panel forecast is based on opinion, output data are somewhat vague. Sales force estimates can be more concrete if the representatives have actually questioned customers as to their future buying intentions. However, neither method is considered good for the identification of turning points.

13

Data Required. The minimum of data required for a panel forecast are two sets of reports over time; information obtained from experts in these reports is presented openly in meetings to enable the forecasters to arrive at a consensus. For sales force estimation, guidelines and past sales data usually help in making accurate projections with only one phase in the process.

Applications. As with other judgmental methods, the consensus opinion technique is best used for forecasts of new product sales and forecasts of margins. Consensus opinion is effective when sales variables do not exhibit stable relationships or when sales are sensitive to factors that are not easily quantified.

 ## Survey of Users

Description. A successful polling of users can be a very helpful step in the development of a firm's sales forecasts. Such polling can minimize many of the potential problems of new product introduction. Information can be gathered through formal market research studies or a company's field sales force. In many companies, part of a salesman's job is to prepare estimates of future sales in his territory. Often these estimates are based on informal, or formal, surveys of major clients that are reflections of the clients' product-purchase intentions.

Outside general purpose surveys are also valued by many forecasters. These surveys can give important clues to future market demand in many industries. Some such surveys include the *McGraw-Hill Survey of Capital Expenditures* and the Conference Board's *Survey of Capital Appropriations*. Surveys of consumer sentiment and buying intentions are also available.

Accuracy. Short term: This method is excellent in the short run because a survey of users reflects their intentions to buy at the time the survey is taken. Long term: Because purchase intentions vary over time in a competitive market atmosphere, a survey of users is only fair in the long run. However, user surveys can be supplemented by additional surveys once a product is on the market.

Cost. A survey of users will often cost several thousands of dollars, though the cost is dependent on the number of people surveyed and the method employed. Many market research firms offer syndicated surveys that are reasonably priced and generate a great deal of data. Informal surveys that use the services of a company's sales force will naturally be less expensive.

Timing. Three months is a reasonable time estimate for a user survey. Professional research firms can turn out surveys in shorter time periods, but they may be more expensive because of short lead times.

Form of Forecast. Data generated from a survey of users are usually very precise and directional. This information can provide a fairly solid basis on which to make forecasting decisions.

Data Required. A minimum of two sets of reports over time is required for this method. The first set is the survey results. The second set relates the survey information to the particular product in question. Information needed includes a considerable amount of market data from surveys, questionnaires, and time series analyses of market variables.

Applications. User surveys are best applied to new product introductions and margin forecasts. One good example of a company that made use of consumer sentiment polls in its forecasting is American Airlines. This firm developed a monthly index based on sample surveys of its passengers. Information obtained from these surveys has allowed American Airlines to predict critical turning points in air travel in recent years. These predictions have enabled management to adjust the company's resources to changing market conditions, achieving significant savings and improved profits.

Heuristic Forecasting

Description. Heuristic forecasting is a forecasting process that uses heuristics, or aids to discovery such as "rules of thumb." The heuristic approach is an attempt to understand the mental operations involved in the thinking process required to develop a forecast.

Heuristic forecasting is the most *subjective* of all forecasting techniques, as its *form* varies, depending on the specific problem. It is ideally suited to two types of problems: those that are too large for traditional research models and those too loosely structured or ill-structured to be expressed in the mathematical terms necessary for the traditional algorithmic models. Surprisingly, many forecasting problems fit into one or the other category.

Essentially, a heuristic forecasting system would attempt to capture the essence of the subjective sales estimating process

15

used by a competent decision-maker and thus approximate the sales estimates made by him. The decision-maker's heuristics would define the program that generates the forecasts. Some of these heuristic programs may be quite simple. However, often they become complex, depending on the forecasting situation and the decision-maker in question.

Accuracy. Short term: Accuracy is quite variable, depending on the exact heuristic program developed. The available applications have shown good accuracy. Long term: Accuracy varies here also. However, accuracy is not as likely to be as great as in the short term because heuristics usually do not take into account situations changed since the heuristics were developed.

Cost. Because heuristic forecasting processes are custom-developed for each situation, heuristic forecasting is very expensive. Heuristic forecasting is usually used when other methods are not applicable.

Timing. Heuristic forecasts usually take one to three months, especially for complex situations. The development of the heuristics requires detailed analysis and interviews of key decision-makers.

Form of Forecast. The output can be presented in any form that the company requires.

Data Required. Most of the heuristics required come from lengthy interviews with decision-makers currently making forecasts without algorithms. The data required are usually the same as used by the decision-makers interviewed.

Applications. Only a few applications are available. One notable example simulated the thinking process of a buyer making estimates by item for a line of merchandise sold by catalog.

CHAPTER V

TIME SERIES TECHNIQUES

Time series techniques rely entirely on historical quantitative data, particularly with respect to the movement over time, and changes of movement over time, of the data. An important assumption to make in choosing these techniques is that past patterns are relevant to predicting future movements. The fundamental purpose of time series techniques is to discern and measure the regular, repetitive patterns of a series of data. Unlike judgmental techniques, these techniques are highly structured; different forecasters applying the same time series techniques to the same data would derive the same forecasts.

The following time series techniques are discussed:

- Trend Fitting

- Moving Average

- Exponential Smoothing

- Adaptive Control

- Box-Jenkins

Trend Fitting

Description. One method of time series analysis is trend-fitting. Basically, this method fits a trend line to a series of deseasonalized sales data. Once this line is established, a forecaster can simply extend it farther to project sales for the future.

A good number of observations are required to identify a trend accurately. Also, if the trend is to be considered alone, it should be viewed in terms of annual data, and the forecast should be projected far enough ahead to minimize cyclical influence.

Trend-fitting is usually a standard feature on computer programs, but it can also be done by freehand plotting or mathematical equations.

If necessary, the forecast by trend-fitting can be adjusted by a relevant seasonal index number to produce the final forecast. Obviously, the easiest solution is to fit a straight line to a data series, but because sales so rarely follow so straightforward a path, non-linear trends must often be explored and used.

Accuracy. Short term: Trend-fitting is considered very good in the immediate short run. It is not, however, effective in identifying turning points. Long term: The method is also considered reasonably good in the long run.

Cost. The cost of trend-fitting varies with application. However, since most of these techniques have been computerized, costs for developing data are usually critical.

Timing. Approximately one day is needed for the application of this method if all the input data are available.

Form of Forecast. Data are produced in quantitative or graph form. The data are very explicit which means that the building of an accurate model is necessary.

Data Required. The data needed vary with the technique used. However, five years' data are a good basis for a reliable forecast.

Applications. Trend-fitting is good for a very wide range of problems, and especially for products in the middle stages of their life cycles. A common application is inventory control on items kept in stock on a regular basis.

Moving Average

Description. Most methods of time series analysis are dependent to some degree on some kind of moving average computed for the subject series. A moving average progresses forward in time as the earliest period included is dropped and the latest one is added. Such an average can be used to (1) make actual forecasts in a direct way; (2) identify the seasonal components in a data series; or (3) smooth out irregular effects of the past to project the future better.

The greater the number of periods used as the basis for the average, the greater is the smoothing effect on the latest data added. To calculate a simple moving average, the value for each period is given equal weight. Sometimes this can be a problem if earlier periods become less relevant to the course of future sales.

In using a moving average directly to forecast future sales, one can sometimes assume that the average for the latest periods will be the value of sales for the period to come. Such a forecast can be made with confidence if a sales series is lacking in volatility; however, this is rarely the case. Usually, the seasonal effects on sales are large enough to require that the forecast be adjusted by an appropriate seasonal index number. The forecasting value then becomes equal to the average sales for the last periods adjusted by the seasonal index for the next period.

Forecasters usually use moving averages in conjunction with other methods. It is especially useful in eliminating or smoothing erratic movements in a data series.

Accuracy. Short term: The moving average is considered good for the immediate short term but poor for the period after that. It does not forecast turning points. Long term: The method is considered quite inaccurate for the long term. This doubtlessly reflects the fact that a data series is rarely so stable that it can be totally forecast with past performance as a basis.

Cost. While a computer is not absolutely necessary in calculating a moving average, most averages are developed using a computer. Many programs exist for calculating moving average forecasts. Data developing costs are important.

Timing. The time required to develop an application and make a forecast is usually one day.

Form of Forecast. The data generated are in quantitative form which is very explicit.

Data Required. At least two years of sales history are needed if seasonal trends are present. The more history used, the better the average will be.

Applications. The moving average is often used for inventory control for standard or low-volume items. For example, a company manufacturing and selling many small items must develop systematic methods of forecasting inventory requirements. To try to forecast sales by each product would be highly impractical. Computer programs are available for systems that provide both perpetual inventory data and updated moving averages. Many catalog houses use moving averages to forecast sales, reorder merchandise and maintain stock levels.

The average can also be used for very short-term sales forecasts: one week, a month, or a quarter at the most.

Exponential Smoothing

Description. Exponential smoothing is directly related to the moving average technique in that it is most appropriately used to forecast a highly stable sales series. However, exponential smoothing obtains a *weighted* moving average. The more recent the observation, the heavier the weight assigned. This is effective when the more recent periods' sales are better predictors of the next periods' sales than those of earlier periods are.

Because the computational process is somewhat burdensome, it is best to use a computer to apply this method. A computer is helpful since one often needs to try several different weighting factors before selecting the one that provides the best forecast.

Exponential smoothing can also allow for trends in sales series by the use of a double exponential smoothing (an ability to capture a linear trend in sales data), and it can deal with the increasing or decreasing of similar trends by using the triple exponential smoothing method. Seasonal movements can be accounted for by using the Winters Method which applies itself to monthly or quarterly data having both seasonal and trend components.

Accuracy. Short term: For immediate forecast periods, exponential smoothing usually provides a highly accurate forecast. Exponential smoothing never forecasts turning points, although it incorporates them faster after their occurrence than does the moving average. Long term: Unfortunately, the method is considered to be very poor in the long run as are all time series analytical methods.

Cost. Costs are low with the use of a computer for exponential smoothing. Obviously, data development costs are important.

Timing. Only one day is required to prepare a forecast using this method if data are available.

Form of Forecast. Again, the data generated from an approach such as this are quantitative. Thus, the data are definitive and easily applied to forecast situations.

Data Required. The data required are the same as for the moving average: at least two years of history if seasonals are present. Otherwise, fewer data are required.

Applications. Exponential smoothing is best used to forecast a highly stable sales series, very similar to the moving average approach. It is often used for inventory control for standard items and short-term sales forecasts.

Adaptive Control

Description. Adaptive control forecasting is similar to exponential smoothing. However, through an iterative process, optimum weights that will reduce the statistical error are derived from historical data. These weights are then used to forecast future demand. With each forecasting period, the actual sales data are used to recalculate the optimal weights. Initially, weights must be estimated to begin the iterative process to calculate optimal weights.

By calculating new weights, adaptive control can provide forecasts more sensitive to historical data than the moving average and exponential smoothing techniques.

Accuracy. Short term: Accuracy is quite good in the short term, especially where sufficiently long series of historical data are available. Accuracy is best with adaptive control when the past data form a relatively smooth or stable pattern. Long term: Accuracy is reasonable in the long term but not as good as in the short term.

Cost. Cost of using adaptive control is higher than exponential smoothing because of the extra computer time needed to calculate optimal weights.

Timing. Timing is similar to using exponential smoothing, except for the additional calculations necessary for the determination of optimal weights.

Form of Forecast. Output is similar to that of exponential smoothing, explicit in either quantitative or graph form.

Data Required. At least two years' data are required. If additional data are available, the technique will work better.

Applications. Many applications of adaptive control exist, especially for forecasting sales demand on a monthly basis.

Box-Jenkins

Description. The Box-Jenkins is a mathematical technique that enables the computer to select the statistical model of the time series that gives the best fit. The computer tests different time series models to determine which one most closely fits the data. The accuracy of the data is therefore equal to the best of the forecasting models from which the computer selects.

The general Box-Jenkins model attempts to account for repeated movements in the historical series, leaving only a series of random movements. The method relies on *auto-regressive* (the stipulation that sales in a certain period are dependent upon sales in previous periods) and *moving average* processes (a concern with past errors in prediction of past sales). The series is adjusted over time by a weighted sum of past errors in estimating sales, both of which account for cyclical seasonal and long-range movements.

The two models—auto-regressive (AR) and moving average (MA)—may be combined to form what is known as an ARMA model. If the data series shows a trend upward, one hopes, the series is called non-stationary; the data must be transformed to yield an ARIMA model, that is, a model with an auto-regressive process and integrated moving average process, using data transformed to be stationary.

Accuracy. Short term: For the immediate short term, the Box-Jenkins model is considered very good to excellent. Beyond the very short term, it loses accuracy in many cases. Long term: For the long term, the Box-Jenkins model does not usually yield accurate forecasts. It is, however, considered fair for the identification of turning points.

Cost. With a computer, the cost may be quite low. However, a computer is not necessary in calculation, in which case cost would depend on man-hours spent.

Timing. The time required to develop an application and make a forecast is one to two days.

Form of Forecast. Data is quantitative and easily applicable to forecasting problems.

Data Required. The data needed for the Box-Jenkins method include a minimum of two years' sales history. However, it is very advantageous to have as much history as possible for model identification.

Applications. The Box-Jenkins method is best used in production and inventory control of large-volume items and for forecasts of cash balances. It is also effective for short-term sales forecasts.

CHAPTER VI

CAUSAL TECHNIQUES

Like time series techniques, causal techniques require historical, quantitative data. Here, however, the data are not merely analyzed for patterns. Instead, relationships between sales and other factors are explicitly sought for and cited. If the causal techniques are used in a pure statistical form, different forecasters will get the same results using different methods. However, in developing the needed relevant causal relationships, different forecasters may add assumed data or judgmental relationships to the available historical data. Depending on the amount of judgmental information used, different results may be obtained from different forecasters.

The following causal techniques are discussed:

- Regression

- Econometric

- Leading Indicator

- Diffusion Index

- Input-Output Analysis

- Life-Cycle Analysis

- Buyer Intentions Surveys

Regression

Description. Perhaps the most widely used causal model for forecasting sales is the regression model. A regression model is an equation that relates sales to independent predictor variables such as level of advertising, the number of salesmen's visits, dollar expended for product promotion, and others. Often it is desirable to understand the relative effect of such variables on the total sales volume expected for the firm. These relationships are primarily analyzed statistically, although the analysis must make rational sense as well.

The equations used are derived either through bivariate or multivariate methods, depending on how many variables are to be analyzed. Bivariate least squares regression analysis involves the fitting of a line to measurements of two variables. The algebraic sum of deviations of the measurements from this line must be zero, and the sum of the squares of the deviations must be less than it would be for any other line. The equation describing this line is, therefore, a mathematical statement of the nature of the relationship between two variables. It can be used to help forecasters understand this relationship, or to predict the values of one of the variables given a value for the second variable.

The general equation for a regression line fitted to two variables is:

$$Y = a + bX$$

where Y is the criterion variable, X the predicting variable, a a constant and b the amount Y changes for each unit of change in X. The regression analysis determines the values of both a and b.

Multivariate methods are techniques involving three or more variables. They are widely used in marketing research because relationships of interest usually involve several variables.

Accuracy. Short term: Accuracy is considered very good in the short run, and identification of turning points is considered reasonable. Long term: Regression analysis is considered only fair in the long run because predictor variables change through time.

Cost. Costs for regression analysis are moderate, especially with the use of a computer. The equations used are not overly complex.

Timing. The time required for regression analysis is approximately one day, once variables are identified and data are available.

Form of Forecast. Output data are in quantitative form and are, therefore, quite explicit. Obviously, data generated from this approach will only be as good as the data from which they are derived.

Data Required. Data used can be sales by region or any other convenient unit over time, as well as the values of predictor variables. At least twenty observations are needed for acceptable results.

Applications. Regression models are usually used in the prediction of overall market demand for a generic product type, rather than for direct prediction of the future volume of an individual company's sales. There are two reasons for this: (1) such modeling generally yields better results with more aggregated data, and (2) a single company seldom exerts more control over total market demand. Once future demand for an overall market is determined by regression methods, a company can use other methods to determine what its own participation in that demand is likely to be.

Econometric

Description. Econometrics may be defined as the application of regression analysis to business and economic problems. An econometric model is a system of interdependent regression equations that describes an area of economic or profit activity. The equations provide simplifications of measureable relationships between the changes in the sales series being forecast, for example, and the changes in other related factors whose values are considered easier to forecast than those of future sales. Because of the interaction of the equations in such models, econometric methods will better express causalities involved than ordinary regression equations.

To use econometrics properly, a forecaster must have a good understanding of the statistical basis of the technique and of economic theory as it relates to both the market being studied and the economy in general. The model-builder must also understand the characteristics of the industry being studied.

The first step in building an econometric model is to identify the potentially influential factors whose changes may be closely associated with changes in the variable to be forecast. Building such a model calls for sound judgment. There are many options to be weighed, and forecasters cannot know for certain which specific variables might prove most promising.

Accuracy. Short term: Accuracy of the econometric model is considered very good to excellent in the short run. It is expected that econometric models which are susceptible to systematic evaluation and improvement will outperform judgmental forecasts in the near future. Long term: The econometric model is considered good in the long run. The identification of turning points is considered excellent in all time frames.

Cost. Econometric models are expensive to develop and can easily cost many thousands of dollars, depending on how "in-depth" they are. Problems of statistically estimating appropriate values of predictor variables are magnified in the dynamic economic environment of individual firms.

Timing. At least two months should be allowed for the development of an econometric model; more complicated models have taken years.

Form of Forecast. The data derived from this method will be in quantitative form and, therefore, quite explicit.

Data Required. The data required are similar to those required for the regression model: sales and values of predictor variables by region, as well as over time. For acceptable results, one needs twenty or more observations.

Applications. As with regression models, econometric models are most often used in the prediction of the overall market demand for a generic product type. It is a rare company that has so dominant a market position that it can regress its own sales history against one or more national economic indicators.

One example of a company that made good use of an econometric model is RCA. Its forecasters learned that quarterly movements of real GNP led the movement of manufacturers' quarterly sales of color television sets to dealers.

Recently econometric models of the economy have not yielded satisfactory results because drastic changes in the economy, such as fuel shortages and record high interest rates, were not anticipated when the models were built.

Leading Indicator

Description. A leading indicator is a time series of an economic activity whose movement in a certain direction precedes the movement of another time series in the same direction. A company that has products with dependent relationships on variables whose changes precede changes in the firm's sales can make profitable use of leading indicators. For example, a baby-food manufacturer found that a good leading indicator of non-milk baby-food sales was the number of births in each area for the past three years, lagged by six months.

Unfortunately, most companies do not have such directly dependent product relationships. Consequently, leading indicators are most often used to forecast changes in overall business conditions rather than to predict sales for individual companies. General business conditions affect the level of sales for most companies.

Data on 40 different time series that are considered to lead the overall economy are collected and published monthly by the Department of Commerce. Included in these indicators are new business formations, new orders in durable goods industries, new building permits, prices of 500 common stocks, and industrial materials prices.

Two problems are inherent in the use of these indicators in forecasting. First, a forecaster often obtains "mixed signals" from the use of such indicators because often they do not all agree. Second, there is the problem of "false signals." Even though most indicators have reasonably good records of predicting turning points that do occur, many often predict turning points that never occur.

Accuracy. Short term: The accuracy for leading indicators is considered good in the short run. Long term: Unfortunately, accuracy is considered quite poor for leading indicators in the long run. This is due to the constantly changing conditions in modern economies.

Cost. With the use of a computer, costs can be moderately high. Obviously, cost depends on how many indicators are used and to what depth they are applied.

Timing. About two weeks to a month is required for a forecast using leading indicators, including data analysis.

Form of Forecast. Output is produced in quantitative form and, therefore, is very explicit.

Data Required. The indicators published by U.S. government agencies and several years' data, in order to relate these indicators to company sales, are needed.

Applications. Leading indicators forecasting is used most often for forecasts of sales by product class or for forecasts of changes in overall business conditions.

Diffusion Index

Description. The diffusion index is the percentage of a group of economic indicators that is going up or down. An index number of 100 means that all indicators have risen; a number of 0 means that all have fallen. For example, a succession of low index numbers over a number of months in an expansionary period should precede an economic downturn. The diffusion index is one method of dealing with the problems of "mixed" and "false" signals involved in the use of leading indicators.

Accuracy. Short term: Accuracy is fair in the short run. Long term: As with leading indicator analysis, accuracy is considered poor in the long run.

Cost. With the use of a computer, costs can be moderately high.

Timing. Approximately one month is required for a diffusion index forecast.

Form of Forecast. As with the leading indicator method, output is in quantitative form and, therefore, is very explicit.

Data Required. Several years' data are usually required to relate company sales to indexes used.

Applications. This method can be used for forecasting sales of overall product classes.

Input-Output Analysis

Description. This method of analysis is concerned with the inter-industry or interdepartmental flow of goods or services in the economy, or a company and its markets. An inter-industry sales ledger, known as an input-output table, has been produced for some 370 industries in the United States. It is a 370 X 370 matrix that shows sales within each industry and to other industries.

This table and others that have been derived from it have mainly been used for forecasting at the level of the overall economy rather than at the level of the individual firm. The tables are particularly useful in evaluating the effects of a change in demand in one industry on other industries. For example, consider that a gasoline shortage is expected to result in a 15 percent decrease in the number of automobiles produced in the upcoming year. This decline in demand will result in a decrease in sales of steel, iron ore, limestone, coal and electricity. A plastics company might use input-output analysis to determine how it would also be affected in this instance.

For individual company forecasts, input-output tables are limited to industrial products and to fairly broad product groupings. In addition, there are two problems with input-output analysis: (1) the data in the tables are not very recent, and (2) the level of aggregation is high. Most companies using the tables have found the industry designations too broad to be useful, thus forcing them to develop additional data at their own expense. When this technique is used, however, the companies that benefit from its use have almost always been large companies.

Accuracy. Short term: In the immediate short run this method is not applicable. However, after about three months the information obtained is considered good in accuracy. Long term: Data gathered in input-output analysis are very good in the long run. This is probably a result of the fact that inter-industry transaction patterns change slowly, as evidenced by a comparison of tables from different time periods. Identification of turning points, however, is considered only fair.

Cost. Corporations have spent as much as $100,000 or more annually to develop useful applications of input-output models. Costs are high because considerable efforts must be made to use input-output models properly, and additional information is often necessary if they are to be applied to specific businesses.

Timing. An approximate time span of six months is usually required for the use of input-output analysis. This technique requires more time than any other forecasting method.

Form of Forecast. The output is quantitative.

Data Required. Ten or fifteen years' history and considerable amounts of information on product and service flows within an economy, or corporation, for each year for which an analysis is desired are needed. Also, basic data developed by the U.S. Department of Commerce and updated every five years are necessary.

Applications. This method is useful only for forecasting sales of industrial products and services. Large companies benefit most from this forecasting method because the industry designations are broad.

Life-Cycle Analysis

Description. This method of forecasting of new product growth is based on S-curves. Central to the analysis are the phases of product acceptance by the various groups such as innovators, early adapters, early majority, late majority and laggards.

Usually, a growth curve is estimated for the product. As sales data are collected the curve is revised. Forecasts are made by reading future points along the S-curve.

Accuracy. Short term: Accuracy is considered good after the initial three-month period. Long term: Accuracy is fair in the long term.

Cost. Costs are moderate in this method although analysis can still be quite detailed.

Timing. One month or more is necessary for life-cycle analysis.

Form of Forecast. The output is quantitative.

Data Required. The annual sales of the product being considered or of a similar product is the minimum requirement. It is also often necessary to conduct market surveys to define the proper S-curve to use.

Applications. Life-cycle analysis is best used for forecasts of new product sales.

Buyer Intentions Surveys

Description. Buyer intentions surveys measure buyer intentions with regard to certain durable goods. They are also used to derive indexes that measure the public's general feeling about the present and the future and to estimate how this feeling will affect buying habits. Usually, these surveys are more effective for tracking and warning rather than forecasting, because turning points are sometimes signaled incorrectly.

Many companies and agencies conduct periodic surveys of buyer intentions. Several surveys of planned business plant and equipment expenditures are conducted, including those taken by McGraw-Hill Publishing Company, the National Industrial Conference Board, the Securities and Exchange Commission, and *Fortune* magazine. Surveys of consumer durables are conducted for public use by the Survey Research Center, the University of Michigan, Consumers Union, and others.

It has been suggested that forecasts of industrial products provided by surveys have been much more useful than those of consumer products. For example, the Department of Commerce survey of new plant and equipment expenditures had an average error of less than 3 percent for the period of 1948 through 1969. In contrast, the *Consumer Buying Expectations Survey* has been discontinued by the Bureau of the Census since 1973 because data users and analysts found it only "marginally useful."

Accuracy. Short term: This method is rated good in the short run. Long term: In the long run, however, this method is rated poor. This poor rating is most likely due to the fact that people's intentions to buy change rapidly.

Cost. Buyer intention surveys are relatively expensive because it is necessary to conduct interviews with consumers.

Timing. Several weeks' time is required for a forecast based on buyer intention surveys.

Form of Forecast. Depending on the method used to gather the data, output information can be fairly explicit and in quantitative form. For privately conducted surveys, formal methodologies will produce the most useful information.

Data Required. Several periods of data are needed to determine the relationship of intentions to company sales.

Applications. This method is typically used for sales forecasting of product classes.

CHAPTER VII

COMPARISON OF TECHNIQUES

The various techniques have been summarized in a Forecasting Decision Matrix. (See following pages.) Each technique is ranked against similar techniques as to the criteria posed by the five forecasting questions: accuracy, cost, timing, form and data. These rankings allow a decision-maker to compare the techniques quickly and focus on the few that should be considered in more detail.

THE FORECASTING DECISION MATRIX

Techniques	Accuracy: Why Do You Need the Forecast?	Cost: How Much Money Is Involved?	Timing: When Will the Forecast Be Used?
Judgmental	*Rankings* (High Accuracy ↔ Low Accuracy) Delphi Survey of Users Consensus Opinion Heuristic Case History/Analogy Expert Opinion	*Rankings* (Low Cost ↔ High Cost) Expert Opinion Consensus Opinion Case History/Analogy Survey of Users Heuristic Delphi	*Rankings* (Short Lead Times ↔ Long Lead Times) Expert Opinion Consensus Opinion Case History/Analogy Survey of Users Heuristic Delphi
Time Series	(High Accuracy ↔ Low Accuracy) Box-Jenkins Adaptive Control Exponential Smoothing Moving Average Trend Fitting	(Low Cost ↔ High Cost) Trend Fitting Moving Average Exponential Smoothing Adaptive Control Box-Jenkins	(Short Lead Times ↔ Long Lead Times) Trend Fitting Moving Average Exponential Smoothing Adaptive Control Box-Jenkins
Causal	(High Accuracy ↔ Low Accuracy) Input-Output Analysis Econometric Diffusion Index Leading Indicator Regression Buyer Intentions Surveys Life-Cycle Analysis	(Low Cost ↔ High Cost) Regression Leading Indicator Diffusion Index Life-Cycle Analysis Buyer Intentions Surveys Econometric Input-Output Analysis	(Short Lead Times ↔ Long Lead Times) Regression Leading Indicator Diffusion Index Life-Cycle Analysis Buyer Intentions Surveys Econometric Input-Output Analysis

Techniques	Form: Who Will Use the Forecast?		Data: How Much Are Available?	
	Precise Forecast ←→ Imprecise Forecast	*Rankings* Survey of Users Heuristic Expert Opinion Consensus Opinion Delphi Case History/Analogy	Considerable Data Required ←→ Little Data Required	*Rankings* Generally, All Similar; Little Historical Data Needed
Judgmental				
Time Series	Precise Forecast ←→ Imprecise Forecast	All Similar, Giving Precise Forecasts.	Considerable Data Required ←→ Little Data Required	All Similar; At Least Two Years Data Usually Required
Causal	Precise Forecast ←→ Imprecise Forecast	All Similar, Giving Precise Forecasts.	Considerable Data Required ←→ Little Data Required	Input-Output Analysis Econometric Life-Cycle Analysis Diffusion Index Leading Indicator Regression Buyer Intentions Surveys

CHAPTER VIII

FORECASTING EFFECTIVENESS

At the outset five forecasting problem areas—mystique, accuracy, consistency, accountability, and implementation—were described. By knowing what questions to ask and by knowing the merits of each technique, the decision-maker should be able to choose the technique that will generate an appropriate forecast. However, true effectiveness in forecasting can be achieved if the decision-maker remains aware of these five problem areas and continually is on guard against them. Words of advice are offered against each problem.

Mystique: Be Approachable

While many forecasters enjoy nurturing the mystique of their specialty, this practice does not serve them well. Instead, forecasters should do all they can to eliminate the mystique. By being more approachable, they will be more valuable to their companies. A few do's and don'ts are suggested:

- Do explain all techniques used—and explain them in simple terms.

- Don't use jargon.

- Do use official names but recognize that others may not be familiar with those names.

- Do be judicious in using computer forms and printouts.

Accuracy: Be Reasonable

Forecasts can be most useful when they are objectively formulated and reasonably presented. Again, the formulation of forecasts needs to be explained. Where possible, the "precise" forecast should be accompanied by a likely range of forecasts, thus giving forecast users a "feel" for the accuracy of the forecast.

Consistency: Be Objective

Keep bias separate. For example, if shading downward for conservatism is appropriate or if compensating upward for a salesperson's consciousness of quota is necessary, do it. However, keep adjustments clearly separate rather than part of the pure forecasting technique. Also, explain the adjustments.

Accountability: Be Involved

Accountability in forecasting is possible if decision-makers are involved in all aspects of the forecasting process. For example, while decision-makers do not need to collect the data themselves, they should know what data are being collected and how they are being used. The same is true for other aspects of the forecasting process, from choosing the technique to presentation of results.

While accountability for forecasting will probably never be completely resolved, problems can be minimized by the involvement of all concerned in the forecasting process.

Implementation: Keep Forecasting Dynamic

Forecasting works best when it is an integral part of the marketing process. Instead of being only an input, forecasting should be used throughout the marketing process. Keeping forecasters informed of progress can lead to valuable contributions and timely update of forecasts. Many decision-makers have been surprised by the valuable contributions forecasters can make in related areas such as quota-setting and sales achievement analysis.

2602

CHAPTER IX

SUMMARY

The objective of this monograph has been to make the decision-maker feel comfortable in choosing the most effective forecasting technique. This confidence should come from three sources:

- Knowing how to approach a forecasting situation by using the five forecasting questions:

  1. Accuracy: Why do you need the forecast?

  2. Cost: How much money is involved?

  3. Timing: When will the forecast be used?

  4. Form: Who will use the forecast?

  5. Data: How much are available?

- Knowing what techniques are available and the advantages of each one. Here, the Forecasting Decision Matrix (page 34) can be a useful tool in helping the decision-maker compare techniques as forecasting situations arise.

- Finally, knowing that effective forecasting minimizes the five forecasting problem areas of mystique, accuracy, consistency, accountability and implementation.